TEENS SPEAK
GIRLS AGES 16 to 18

Sixty Original Character Monologues

by Kristen Dabrowski

KIDS SPEAK SERIES

A Smith and Kraus Book

A Smith and Kraus Book
Published by Smith and Kraus, Inc.
177 Lyme Road, Hanover, NH 03755
www.smithkraus.com

© 2005 by Kristen Dabrowski
All rights reserved.

First Edition: March 2005
Manufactured in the United States of America
10 9 8 7 6 5 4 3 2 1

Cover and text design by Julia Gignoux, Freedom Hill Design

Library of Congress Cataloging-in-Publication
Dabrowski, Kristen.
Girls speak, ages 16-18 : sixty original character monologues / by Kristen
Dabrowski.-- 1st ed.
p. cm. -- (Kids speak series)
ISBN 1-57525-414-X
1. Monologues. 2. Acting. I. Title: Girls speak, ages sixteen to eighteen. II. Title:
Girls speak, ages sixteen through eighteen. III. Title. IV. Series.

PN2080.D336 2005
812'.6--dc22

2004059102

CONTENTS

Many thanks to Eric and Marisa

Foreword

Hello, actors! Inside this book, you'll find sixty monologues for girls aged 16 to 18.

Here's how they are organized:

- There are six sections in the book. Each section includes ten monologues from the point of view of one character. Each character is described on her own introduction page.

- Each character was designed to have different experiences and views on the world. You'll see her in school, at home, with strangers, etc.

How to choose a monologue:

- You may want to begin by looking at the character descriptions. Choose a character most like you or, for a challenge, choose one that is quite different from yourself.

- Page through the monologues. There are dramatic, comic, and semicomic monologues in each section. Some characters tend to be more comic or dramatic than others.

- Trust your instincts!

How to perform the monologues:

- Tell your story clearly.

- Know to whom you're speaking and imagine you are talking to just that one person. (Of course, if you're talking to more people, keep that in mind as well!)

- A new paragraph or *(Beat.)* means that there is a pause due to a subject change or another (imaginary) person speaking. Be sure that you know what the unseen person is saying.

- Play around with the monologue and try doing it a lot of different ways.

Have fun!

Kristen Dabrowski

SERENA STEWART

Serena is a flirt and a party girl. She doesn't like to take life seriously and lives by the motto "I'll try anything once."

THE DREAM

Serena, comic
At a friend's house, talking to her best friend.

Those shoes go fine with that outfit! Enough already! You've had on six tops and four skirts, a pair of jeans, and three pairs of shoes. It doesn't matter, OK? We are going to a party. No one is going to even *look* at your shoes. It will be *dark*. Come on! This is taking the fashionably late entrance too far. In so so many ways.

I want to actually *go* to the party. If people are looking at your shoes, there's a problem. Everyone should just be having fun. What's wrong with this society? How did we go so wrong? What happened to the days when people flirted, smoked, drank, made out, and just enjoyed not having parents around? How did we get so shallow?

Now I'm depressed. Thanks a lot. *(Beat.)* You're ready? You're sure? *(Beat.)* Of course I still want to go. Are you kidding? Let's get out of here before you change your mind!

REPUTATION

Serena, comic
At school, talking to a friend.

Do you think I'm slutty? *(Beat.)* I know I'm not. But I wonder if other people know. I mean, you have to test guys out, know what I mean? So I've made out with a lot of guys. It's important to know what you're getting into, and it's not as if I sleep around. I mean, take Saturday's party, for example. I made out with two guys at the same party, so people are saying stuff about me. What people don't know is that I've liked Matt and Jake forever. Of course it would be just my luck that they would both *finally* make their move on the same night!

And it's not like I could just choose to kiss one of them. I had to do research in order to make an informed choice.

What do you mean which did I choose? I still don't know. It was kind of even. Jake is cuter and Matt is cooler. And they both kiss pretty well. I'm going to have to do more homework. I think that is the first and last time you'll ever hear me say that sentence!

ALL PLAY AND NO WORK

Serena, comic
At work, talking to a coworker.

I actually like this job. I swear. I mean, not the work part, but you get to meet so many people. Take you, for instance. I'm totally glad I know you. Aren't you? I think we really mesh, don't you? I love talking to you. And the tips! Don't you love the tips? I get the best tips. You just have to be a little nice to people, and most of the time they're cool about it. Every once in a while you get one of those old people who leave you a quarter or something, but most of the time . . . You are so easy to talk to!

Would we even talk to each other if we went to the same school? I don't know. Maybe, maybe not. And that's what makes this situation so cool.

You go to college, right? That is so cool. Do you have a girlfriend? Would you want to take me out sometime? I mean, somewhere other than here, of course. Somewhere good.

Yeah, I know what I said. I *do* like to work here. But there's no way I'm eating this food.

TESTY

Serena, comic
At school, talking to a friend.

Honest to God, I failed that test. And you can't even fail the SAT. But that's how bad I did. I don't even think I filled in the right circles for my name. What happens if I get, like, a 150 out of 1600 or something? What's the worst possible thing that could happen? Could I still get into a party school? Because that's all I want to do. No one even uses their college education anyway, do they? Everyone majors in, like, things like sociology and stuff, and then they become newscasters or something. So why do we even go through all this? It's a colossal joke. It's a scam to make money. How did they get *all* the kids in the country to do this? Whose idea was it? I object! I'm going to sue . . . someone! God, I just hate the whole world!

I hate school anyhow. Who needs it? I'll just live at home, and mooch off my parents for another decade or two.

Oh, God, I have to get a good score on this stupid test or my life is over!

ENVELOPE NO. 1

Serena, dramatic
At school, talking to her best friend.

I can't open it. I can't. I'm too scared. What if my score is horrible? What if it's totally embarrassing? Should I lie? Would you lie? It's not as if you'd have to. I'm sure your score is amazing.

How about you open my envelope and I open yours? Then we can break the news to each other. OK?

(Mimes opening a letter.) You did really well! Of course! You got a 1200. At least I think so! I'm sure my math score is so bad I can't even add right. So . . . what's mine?

A what? A . . . 1450? No. No. Is my name on it? Me? But . . . you're the smart one! Maybe they got switched.

No, no, Hayley, don't get upset! Your score is really good! Mine is just . . . dumb luck or something!

SUPERIOR

Serena, dramatic
At school, talking to a friend.

Everyone's treating me different. It's weird. Sometimes I like it, sometimes I don't. Like teachers are thinking I'm smart now. Who knows? Maybe I am. I never really thought about it. Maybe I really do have "potential." I just hope they don't start expecting things from me. I don't know how smart people do it. It's stressful just thinking about it.

And Hayley is acting really weird. It's like she's mad at me for doing better than her. I mean, before we even got our scores I was saying how dumb these tests are. I'm sure the SATs don't measure intelligence. I mean, when in life are you going to have to apply things like "hatchet is to scythe as hedgehog is to cucumber" or whatever. I'm sure this stuff never comes up. It seems like a really lame reason for your best friend to be mad at you. It's not like I *did* anything.

I'm mad at her, actually. What the hell? Hayley can be such a wench, I swear. And I should know. I got a 1450 on my SATs.

RESPONSIBILITY

Serena, semicomic
At home, talking to her sister.

Listen, young lady, you'll do what I say. Because I'm in charge here. No monkey business, you hear me? Behave yourself! And be careful. I don't want to be taking you to the emergency room.

I do not sound like Mom! No way! Impossible. I'm in charge of taking care of you this afternoon and I'm . . . I *have* to sound more adult than usual. That's all. But I *don't* sound like Mom.

I was taking special care *not* to sound like Mom, so don't give me this "you've turned into Mom" crap! Jeez, you're just a stupid little kid. You don't know what I sound like! *(Beat.)* You are not going to tell Mom I called you stupid. Or that I said "crap." Those are not bad words. You have no idea. *(Beat.)* Listen, I said you're not saying anything, so you're not, young lady. You stop that *right now*. I've had enough of you! Go to your room and think about what you've done!

ENVELOPE NO. 2

Serena, semicomic
At home, talking to her mother.

Oh. Thanks. Wait! Is it big or small, Mom? The envelope! Is it big or small? I am not getting snotty; this is how I talk. Listen, can you just answer the question?

What do you mean, you don't know? You must know. Just guesstimate. Forget it! Give me the envelope! *(Sighs.)* Please.

It's small. No, it's more than one page, I think. That's good, right? If I don't get in, I'm just going to die! I can't open it. You open it. Please.

You have to! I can't take this! *(Beat.)* Why are you always so cruel? So "tough love"? I just want you to do this one thing for me and you pull the "you're going to have to start doing things for yourself" stuff. Does that—Do you—Do you think I got in then?

Fine! I'll open the envelope myself!

FALLOUT

Serena, dramatic
In her room, talking to a friend.

If I tell you something, do you swear not to tell anyone? Because you're my best friend, Hayley. I have to tell someone. It's just so, so embarrassing. *(Beat.)* No, I'm not pregnant! Gross!

It's that . . . I heard from Hanover. And . . . I didn't get in. Can you believe it? I mean, my SATs were so good, I really thought—

Well, I *know* my grades aren't great, but everyone kept saying my SATs would—

Could you just shut up a minute? I swear, no one cares about my feelings at all. I *know* I haven't been the perfect student, but I got my hopes up because of my scores, and I just started to think . . . you know, that maybe it was possible to go to a really awesome school. I mean, before all this started, I only thought about going to a party school, but the guidance counselors and everything just got me to thinking . . .

Oh, Hayley, I'm so sad! My whole life is ruined now. It's all downhill from here. Please don't criticize me. I get enough of that from my parents. What if I don't get into college at all?

REASONABLE

Serena, semicomic
In her room, talking to a friend.

Don't go there. That school is a total drag. Go where I'm going.
It'll be great! We can room together and go to parties and rush
a sorority—it'll be *so* great! Can't you just see it? Us getting our
books at the student union. Us buying really cute T-shirts with
school emblems. Us getting radically ill after going to our first
frat party. It'll be perfect!

You don't seem excited. You're going to dump me, aren't you?
You want to go to your snotty school in New Hampshire, don't
you? *(Beat.)* I did not want to go there! I thought about it for
about five minutes, then realized how completely un-fun it
would be! *(Beat.)* I *know* I didn't get in. Believe it or not, I'm
not a complete idiot. But I don't care. When I thought about
it—the cold weather, the isolation, the endless schoolwork—I
mean, who needs that when I could be tanning and—

Just don't be a loser, Hayley! You have to come with me to
Florida and that's that.

HAYLEY ZIERA

Hayley is mature, ambitious and has excellent judgment, except when it comes to guys. She tends to make deep connections with a few friends rather than hanging with a crowd.

DISSENT

Hayley, dramatic
At school, talking to a teacher.

Excuse me, Mrs. Grant? I think I got someone else's paper. I mean, this is my paper, but this is not my grade. It's a *D*. I've never gotten a D in my whole life. I worked hard on this paper. There must be a mistake.

You didn't like it? There's almost no red marks on it. Could you give me a clue about what you didn't like? I think I deserve at least that.

You don't agree with my viewpoint. Well, didn't I back up my arguments? I researched everything thoroughly. See? Right here I wrote—

It shouldn't matter if you think my viewpoint is valid. It's about my ability to back up my words and express myself clearly and concisely.

I don't care what you say. You can't do this. I have a right to free speech, even in your classroom. This is an A paper, and I deserve my A. Until *you* can clearly, concisely, and *logically* tell me why I didn't get one, I am just going to stand here at your desk. I don't care if this takes all day.

RANT

Hayley, dramatic
At home, talking to her father.

You can't *agree* with her, Dad! This violates, God, everything about why people *go* to school! You go to learn to think for yourself, right? To be able to, I don't know, open your mind and filter information and learn to analyze things logically— Can't you see how wrong this is? I got *detention* for standing up for what I believe in!

OK, now you're just being technical. I got detention for not going to my next class, but I wasn't *cutting*; I was staging a demonstration. I simply told Mrs. Pigface that I was not going to leave her classroom until she gave me a *good* reason why I got a D on my well-researched, well-thought-out, really excellent paper! Just because she's a Nazi Republican bitch trying to brainwash me—No! Not even that!—trying to *force* her medieval views down the throats of young people doesn't mean I didn't write a great paper.

I am not going to detention! And I refuse to accept this D in history! *And* I cannot believe you are not with me on this! I feel like I'm living in some kind of sick, *1984*-type universe! I hate everyone!

POLITICS

Hayley, semicomic
At school, talking to a classmate.

Listen, Cody, I just can't do that. Really. You'd be surprised how little power the Class President actually holds. *(Beat.)* OK, maybe you wouldn't. But I know for a fact the administration will never go for a DJ in the cafeteria. Who's going to pay for it? And as for letting the Hip-Hop Club go to New York dance clubs, well, it's a permission nightmare. It's just not going to happen.

No; I'm not even going to try. Because it won't work. Do you have any idea how hard it was to get a salad bar in the cafeteria? Really hard. They didn't want to go for it. And that didn't minutely entail any possible lawsuits or anything. I mean, I suppose someone could smash their head on the sneeze guard or something, but it's remote. Do you know they won't let us have coffee because they're afraid someone will burn themselves and sue the school? This is what I'm up against, Cody.

I'm not trying to be a bitch or anything. I just know it's not going to work. Plus, you know if they agree to music in the cafeteria it's going to be, like, Hootie and the Blowfish or something. Think about it.

SATURDAY NIGHT

Hayley, comic
At home, talking to her best friend.

Every time we go to a party together, you end up making out with some guy and I end up standing in a corner with the geekiest guy within four counties. Seriously. Last week, the guy actually had tape on his glasses and wouldn't stop talking about how he loves hunting. He went into great detail about how to skin a rabbit. I nearly puked on him, and I wasn't even drunk.

That's another thing. I just don't like beer. I don't. It tastes like liquid moss or something. It tastes like dirt. I don't get it. I know I'm not supposed to even care what it tastes like, but it's nasty. And when you're the only one not drunk at a party, well, you begin to see how lame and useless life is. It gets really depressing. Everyone just seems really stupid. It's funny for about five minutes, then you start to feel so isolated. You start to feel like a chaperone at a school dance. Like a total loser.

I'm just not cut out for this stuff. I know it makes me a dork, but I'm just not going to this party. Besides, I have nothing to wear.

SUITOR NO. 1

Hayley, semicomic
At school, talking to a classmate.

How can I say this? I like you, Matt. Wait! It's not what you think. I don't *like* you like you. Get what I'm saying? You're nice, and I'd really like to be friends. But I'm just not really—

I'm not frigid! I'm— *(Beat.)* I'm *not* a prude! You don't know me at all! Listen, I don't like you. You're a creep. Do you think I'm stupid? I know you used to go out with Mimi Pimlott and brag about all the "stuff" you'd do. And excuse me if I'm too smart to end up as a school joke. *(Beat.)* It is *not* better to be a slut than a prude—and I'm not a prude! I have self-respect. Does this actually work with other girls? These insults? Do people actually give in to you because you call them names and act like a pig? The thought of you actually touching me gives me the heebie-jeebies—and *not* because I'm a prude or I'm frigid or I'm a lesbian (I know you're warming up to that). I'd rather be dead. I bet you have skid marks in your underwear. Get away from me. You disgust me.

SUITOR NO. 2

Hayley, semicomic
Outside her house, talking to her date.

Yeah, this was a really fun night. I didn't think I'd enjoy watching *Flesh Eating Monsters III*, but it was actually a somewhat amusing parody of the dangers of totalitarianism, wasn't it?

Oh! Thanks for not doing pizza after the movie. You know, after the blood and the flesh eating, I just couldn't face it. So, thanks for being cool about that. Sorry I went on for so long about politics. As you can tell, I'm really into that stuff. I could tell you weren't really . . . informed . . . but we can agree to disagree, right? Or we could even not talk about it at all. We could talk about . . .

Uh, do you know . . . Your . . . um, your hand is on my breast. Do you know that? *(Beat.)* Could you maybe get it off, please? *(Beat.)* I am stunned. Why did you do that? You don't have the right to manhandle me without my permission. *(Beat.)* You thought that was what people *did*? You didn't even kiss me! This is our first date!

I'm going inside. Don't call me.

SUITOR NO. 3

Hayley, comic
At a coffee shop, talking to a guy.

What's it like, college? I'm really excited to go. High school is just so . . . high school. *(Beat.)* I just don't quite connect with people there. Even my best friend, I've sort of outgrown her. I hate to say that, I really do. I still like her, but we really have nothing in common. No one *thinks* about things beyond what party they're going to on Friday night. It's tiresome.

This Friday? At your frat house? Sure. I could go. So you belong to a fraternity? I didn't see you as the type . . .

No, I really don't see myself joining a sorority. I'm not really sure why you need to pay to sing goofy songs and all that. I can do that anyway, right? *(Beat.)* Oh, sure, sisterhood is a good thing. Definitely. But do you see what I'm getting at? It's a big corporation, basically. You're paying for the privilege to have forced socialization. It's not as if you can't make friends on your own, right?

Did I make you mad? I didn't mean to. Maybe I just don't understand. Can we still go out next Friday? I didn't really mean what I said. I was just blabbering. I'm stupid like that sometimes.

THAT NIGHT

Hayley, dramatic
At home, talking to her mother.

Mom, I have to go to this party. I promised Serena I'd go with her. She's depending on me. We're going to sort of protect each other. So, without me, she's on her own at a college party. And, basically, all we wanted to do is just see what college is like. We just want to interview some people about their college experience. It's research.

Mom! This is important! My whole future is based on this party! It won't be the same just taking college tours. This is a way to hear the *real* story, not some propaganda the school made up!

Don't you trust me? We aren't just going to hook up with college guys. And we're not going to drink. I don't do that stuff. Come on! I *have* to go! I'm *going* to go! You have no reason not to let me! I promised I would go, and I'm going! You are not going to ruin my integrity because you think I'm a little girl. You can't control me forever. I'm old enough to do whatever I want.

TREADING WATER

Hayley, dramatic
At a party, talking to a guy.

Hi, Bryan! Remember me? Hayley? We met at the coffee shop? You asked me to come tonight? *(Beat.)* Yeah, I was the one who . . . sometimes I let my mouth get away from me! But you shouldn't listen to everything I say. So . . . this is fun! It's good to see you. How have you been?

Am I in your way or something? It just seems like you're trying to look past me. Are you . . . embarrassed to see me? 'Cause you *asked* me to come. Never mind. I'll just go. I don't know why I came. I thought you asked . . . Whatever. I guess I'm just some dumb high school kid to you.

(Begins to walk away.) What? Sure, I'd like a drink. But not if it's too much trouble. *(Beat.)* This really is a great place. I can see why you like it so much. This is definitely where I want to go to college. I really appreciate you showing me around. I was going to go to Hanover, but now I see . . . This place is so much better.

SUITOR NO. 3 REDUX

Hayley, semicomic
At a coffee shop, talking to a friend.

He asked me out again, Serena! He is so cute. *(Beat.)* My mom? I'm just not going to tell her he's in college. She's so weird about that. First of all, as if age matters. Second of all, he's only two years older than me. That's nothing. And girls are so much more mature than guys anyway.

Bryan Grossman . . . it's such a perfect name, isn't it? I can't wait to see him again! Serena— *(A stranger interrupts.)*

Oh, hi. Yeah, I said Bryan Grossman. *(Beat.)* Do you know him? *(Beat.)* Yeah, he has brown hair and hazel eyes. He's really cute. He's a sophomore— *(Beat.)* Well . . . yeah, he's my boyfriend. Why? *(Beat.)* He can't be *your* boyfriend. He asked me out *again* just yesterday. He never said . . . It's got to be a different guy. *My* Bryan Grossman wouldn't . . .

Oh my God, Serena! I hate men!

MADDY LYNN SOAMES

Maddy Lynn is bursting with energy and good vibes. She has small town values and respects her elders. Maddy Lynn has a clear vision of her future and is determined to see it through.

PSYCHED

Maddy Lynn, comic
At school, talking to a classmate.

I am so psyched about today's game! Can you stand it? *(Beat.)* Sorry to have *school spirit*. Why are you always such a downer? We don't know each other, but you must get excited about *something*. Think fast—what makes you happy? *(Beat.)* I don't believe you. Something must make you happy. For example, I love summer and going to the beach and my lip gloss in Bee Stung Blush and standing up in front of the whole school and—

Honestly, I don't get you. Maybe this is why— Maybe I shouldn't say this, but I really think it might help. People are a little scared of you. And not in a "oh, she's so tough" way. In a "what's wrong with her" way. I'm not judging. I think there is room in the world for everyone. Your tattoo is wicked, by the way. But you keep to yourself and you're always down. Reach out! People will embrace you, I'm sure.

Gosh, you're funny. No one's going to give you a disease! If they do, you're definitely embracing the wrong people! Now, please, Methodone, tell me *one thing* that makes you happy!

MATCHMAKER

Maddy Lynn, comic
In a diner, talking to a friend.

Keith, I want some ice cream. Pleeeeease? It's important to me, Keithie. Don't you love me? I know you do. Pleeeeease?

Thank you, sweetie! When Dylan and I break up, if we ever break up, which we won't, I am so going to snatch you up. You're such a catch. That's why I love you so much. You know how to treat a girl right. In fact, I'm going to get you a girlfriend. What do you like in a girl? Like looks or personality traits.

Red hair? Be serious! I'm asking an important question. You like girls with my color hair, right? *(Beat.)* I thought so. I'll write it down: golden chestnut with blond highlights. And eyes? *(Beat.)* Blue eyes? Do you mean blue-green like mine? *(Beat.)* My eyes are not brown! I can't believe you thought that! We've known each other for so long. I thought you knew me better than anyone. *(Beat.)* No, I'm not *offended.* I'm just *surprised.* But let's move on. Should she have a bubbly personality, a person who makes other people happy?

"Not too much." How can a person be too "up"? How about Methodone Schwartz with all her black, saggy clothes? Or is she too up for you, too? Just forget it, Keith. You're not making any sense.

STANDARDS

Maddy Lynn, semicomic
In a car, talking to her boyfriend.

Dylan, my lips are sore. I can't kiss you anymore. I need time for them to recover. I already tried telling my dad that I was using this new lip gloss, Lip Venom, that's supposed to make your lips puffy, but I don't think he bought it. Even though there *is* such a product.

Don't pout. You know I want to kiss you. It would help if you shaved a little better. I swear I get stubble burn. *(Beat.)* No! Tomorrow I need to be hickey-free. My dress for the wedding scene is so beautiful, and my neck and shoulders are completely exposed. *(Beat.)* Maria used to be a nun, Dylan. She is not going to have hickeys on her neck on her wedding day.

Why are you getting so pushy? We are saving ourselves, remember? We signed a paper and I plan to keep my promise to God. If you want to get struck down by lightning for lying to God, you just keep it up. *(Beat.)* Fine. Five more minutes. But no hickeys!

HORMONES

Maddy Lynn, semicomic
At a clothing store, talking to a friend.

Keith, how does this look on me? Is it too small? I think it might be too small. Be honest. I can take it. You know, I think my boobs have grown this year. Do you think so? It's OK to say so. *(Beat.)* No? I'm actually sure they have; I've gone up a cup size. My cups runneth over! Do you think I could be a model? *(Beat.)* I know I'm not that tall, but neither is Kate Moss. Actually, it doesn't even matter. I want to be an actress. Do you think I could be an actress? *(Beat.)* I think so, too, Keithie! You are so sweet.

Listen, can I talk to you about something personal? Lately, Dylan is totally horny. Really. You know that paper we signed about being virgins 'til we're married? Dylan is starting to say things like it's unnatural and talking about what things he thinks that includes and which things it doesn't include. And I just don't know. I have urges, Keith; I do. I'm human. But I just have this picture of my wedding day and I don't want to mess it up. What do you think? *(Beat.)* Break up with him? Isn't that extreme?

Well, this shirt is definitely out because I look too sexy in it. I don't want to drive Dylan *completely* crazy.

BRAND-NEW CAR

Maddy Lynn, comic
At home, talking to her father.

I don't really think I want to drive. It's a little scary. I just don't know if I could handle all the cars speeding past me. You'll take me anywhere I want to go, Daddy, right?

I know it's an important skill, but I'm scared. I'll just have to find a husband eventually to take me places. But 'til then I have you. Anyway, I'm not going to get my own car even after I get my license, am I? I'd have to borrow your car all the time, and I know you'd hate that. That car is your baby. Sometimes I think you love it more than any person on the planet. What if I crashed it? Wouldn't you just hate me forever? I couldn't do that to you. And if you hated me, I don't know what I'd do! So, as long as you don't mind driving me to the mall and to school and to practices and to my friends' houses—

You'll talk to Mom about getting me a car? Can it be red? Please, not an old lady car. I wouldn't drive it; I swear I wouldn't! *(Beat.)* Oh, Daddy, you're the best! I love you so much!

THE STAGE

Maddy Lynn, comic
At a friend's house, talking to a friend.

There's just something about having the lights on you and everyone looking at you, fascinated, curious. It's intense. Don't you
feel it? I just love it. I don't know how it can scare you. Honestly. But we can work on it. I can help; I'm sure of it.

The thing is, Ashley, it's not *you* up there. It's you, but it's not,
if you get my meaning. It's more than you. You're playing a character. You don't wear your clothes, you have stage makeup on
. . . When I'm onstage, it's like I go to another place, where I'm
brave and bold and not afraid of anything. If people don't like
you, it's not *you*. It's the script or the director or whatever. And
it's like you just drink in the energy of the audience. How can
you not love that? You get to be anything or any way you want.
I mean, I'm supernice, right? But onstage I can be wicked and
mean and just get all that out. It's such a release!

Ashley, you need to not be so self-centered. It's not about you.
No one cares about you when you're onstage. It's all about the
character. You are merely a vessel. A glamorous, beautiful vessel that everyone's staring at.

Don't you feel better?

CULTURE CLUB

Maddy Lynn, comic
At school, talking to a friend.

That's tacky, Janine. You can't just shovel your food in your mouth like that. It makes you look like a pig.

I'm not saying you *are* a pig, just that you look like one when you eat. I'm just embarrassed to be around you; that's all. It's not a reflection on who you are as a person. That's why I'm telling you. It's something you can fix.

I'd think it would be something you'd want to consider. After all, you complain all the time that you don't have a boyfriend, that guys don't want to ask you out. I'm just trying to be a *friend*. I'm trying to *help*. It might significantly increase your popularity if you sit up when you eat and use your knife and fork properly—to bring the *food* to *you*, not *you* to the *food*. You might actually look like a girl, not a caveman.

I *know* spaghetti is messy. That's why you never order spaghetti in public, Janine. This is a commonly known fact. It's undignified. And nothing's worse when you're trying to impress a guy than tomato sauce dripping down your face and—oh, God, stop it!—that slurping sound.

Don't argue with me, Janine. I know what I'm talking about.

JEALOUS

Maddy Lynn, dramatic
At school, talking to a friend.

You tripped me! You meant to do that! You wanted me to be humiliated in front of the whole school! You're an evil bitch. Oh, God, see what you made me say!

I've known all along that you were jealous of me, Ashley. It's so obvious. Don't even try to pretend it's not true. And to think, I went out of my way to help you. *This* is how you repay me? By tripping me in the middle of my big number? It was *my* moment, Ash, not yours.

You might think or hope that this would make me a joke or a laughingstock, but you're wrong. You can't turn the tide of popularity like that. Everyone will see you for what you are—a spiteful you-know-what. I'll make sure of it. You're ruined!

Maybe I'm not being Christian. But you deserve what you get, you nasty witch.

BREAK

Maddy Lynn, dramatic
At school, talking to her boyfriend.

You what? Excuse me? *(Beat.)* You're so funny, Dylan. *(Beat.)*
Stop joking around! *(Beat.)* You want to break up with me? As
if. No way. We've been together . . . We talked about being together forever. Being each other's firsts. You're not going to
throw that away now.

Stop joking! You're really starting to make me mad. I know you
don't mean it. We're meant to be together, Dylan. We both knew
it the first time we saw each other. You told me that I was the
most beautiful girl in the world. You told me we were going to
get married.

What's this all about? Did someone put you up to this? Did I
do something that made you mad? You can just tell me. I know
I can be a handful sometimes. But that's because I want things
to be perfect with us. We *can* be perfect.

There's no way there's someone else. You can't possibly love
anyone more than me. I refuse to accept this!

THE END OF THE WORLD

Maddy Lynn, semicomic
At home, talking to a friend.

I haven't washed my hair in two days. And that's one day longer than is entirely healthy! I can't get out of bed. I think I'm dying.

My whole world, Janine, my whole entire world has fallen apart. I've based my whole life on the fact that Dylan and I were going to get married. Going to be together forever. Going to get married and have babies and live happily ever after. Then he had to go mess it up. He's not really with *her*, is he? Because I just couldn't bear it. I know now what it's like to be a celebrity, almost.

Well, because when a celebrity has a breakup, they still have to see the other person all the time on billboards and in magazines and at award shows. And they have to smile, pretending it doesn't matter. That's what I have to do with Dylan at school! Even though he's probably sucking face with that horrible whore—I'm sorry to say it, Janine, but it's true—right now!

I can't go back. I'll just have to get my GED or get home schooled. Do you think my parents will move to another district if I ask them? I can't bear to see him. Ever.

ROSA GARCIA-SMITH

Rosa is high-energy and talkative. She is accustomed to the fast-moving, aggressive, outspoken lifestyle of her native New York City, where she lives with her mother.

HOT IN THE CITY

Rosa, comic
Outside, talking to her friend.

Oh, God, Sylvie, I swear that there aren't usually dead rats in the street. This always seems to happen when people are visiting from out of town. The grossest, most disgusting stuff turns up. Puke. Dog crap. Bloody bottles. Most times, it's just normal. Not normal for you maybe, but still . . .

Oh, Lord, it doesn't usually smell this bad either! There's a garbage strike and the restaurant on the corner here, well . . . it's August and what are you gonna do? Just smell your hand. Or mine. My hand lotion smells really strong.

You're never gonna come back, are you, Sylvie? Tell me you will, maybe in fall or winter? It smells *so* much better. I mean, you might see a dead rat or two, but that's the worst of it.

Oh, my God, is that a celebrity? Oh, you must have missed him. I think it was Brad Pitt. *(Beat.)* OK, that was a lie. But I want to give you a good impression!

LASHING OUT

Rosa, comic
At the airport, talking to a security officer.

Are you serious? You're going to go through my luggage? Do I look like a terrorist to you? I'm a kid.

This is embarrassing. Just so you know, I don't have a problem or anything. I'm just going away for a long time. So that's why I have, like, a thousand tampons. I thought it would be less embarrassing than buying them every month. I thought wrong, didn't I?

What are you looking for anyway? My plane is going to be taking off soon. I got here late because, well, my stomach was upset? And I didn't feel so good? Probably because I was leaving and I always get nervous before I have to fly places or when I have to meet new people. So, can I go now?

I swear I don't have any bombs or weapons in here. I swear. Please, hurry! You're going to make me sick to my stomach again. Please, mister!

An eyelash curler. You're taking my eyelash curler. Do you think I'm going to squeeze someone's eyelids to death or something? Never mind, whatever! Can I go now?

BRAVE NEW WORLD

Rosa, comic
At her exchange family's home, talking to her host family.

Hey, I need coffee! *(Beat.)* I know it's hot, but there's such a thing as iced coffee. It's very refreshing. *(Beat.)* Coffee isn't bad for you. I've been drinking it since I was a little girl!

Oh. My. God. Oh, my God. It is going to be the longest school term of my life. I'm already going through withdrawal. Look at me! I'm shaking! I need my fix or I am not going to be a very happy girl!

Am I yelling? I don't think I'm yelling. This is such a strange place. Everyone is, like, shy and polite. Where I come from, everyone is like THIS! Really big and loud!

I'm really sorry. I'm going to try very, very hard to be superquiet. It's just not my nature, you know? It makes me feel like I'm gonna explode when I try to keep things in. But I swear, if you find me some caffeine, I will be so good, you won't even know I'm around.

CONCLUSIONS

Rosa, dramatic
At her exchange family's home, talking to her host mother.

I'm not on drugs, Mrs. Hagenhofer. This is just how I act. How could you think that? I think it's wrong of you to just jump to conclusions like that. You don't know me. Is it because I'm from the city or because I'm not white as a ghost like you?

You think *I'm* rude? You just told me you thought I was on drugs! For no reason! What have I ever done to make you think that? *(Beat.)* So what? I talk fast. I'm high energy. I'm used to going places and doing things, not just sitting around and watching TV night and day. I start to feel cooped up. It makes me a little crazy.

You're not my mother, you know. You can't tell me what to do. I can do what I want. By the way, my mother trusts me to keep out of trouble. I happen to have very good instincts about people. And I'm starting to get an instinct about you, Mrs. Hagenhofer.

I think you are a little bit racist, do you know that?

NOWHERE TO RUN TO

Rosa, dramatic
Outside, talking to a friend.

My host family is like the KKK or something. They kicked me out! Can I stay here?

Do you think I'm on drugs? *(Beat.)* Good, 'cause I'm not. I mean, I've had pot from time to time, but that's nothing serious. I'm a good girl. They should worryabout their stupid son, not me.

I need to unwind. Is there anywhere we can go? *(Beat.)* The mall? Seriously? No way. God, I hate this place! *(Beat.)* Don't get all offended. It's just a fact that this is a slow, boring place. *(Beat.)* What are you getting in my face for?

If you want a fight, I'll give it to you. You people are crazy! I don't know how you survive. Everywhere I go everyone is telling me how I need to calm down. Meanwhile, you all keep picking a fight with me. But if that's the way you want it, I'll wipe the sidewalk with your face. Come and get it!

SURVIVAL CAMP, DAY 1

Rosa, dramatic
In a cabin, talking to strangers.

No way did my mom agree to this. I want to talk to her. You have to let me talk to her! These people are my host family, not my real family. They can't do this to me. I didn't do anything wrong.

I got in a fight, but I was *provoked*. And I called my host mother a racist, but that's because she *was*. She said I was on drugs. It was a blatantly racist comment.

I don't take drugs. *I don't*. I have no idea where the pot came from. It's not mine. Isn't anyone listening? Look, there is no way I am going to give you my shoes and let you dump me in the woods. You call my mother! I'm a good girl! She'll tell you!

I *don't* need to learn respect. I respect authority. You just have no authority over me! I don't know you. How do I know you're not going to kill me? This is a nightmare. Can't anyone help me? I don't understand this! Won't anyone listen to me? This is a huge mistake!

SURVIVAL CAMP, DAY 7

Rosa, dramatic
Outside, talking to a friend.

None of us should be here. No one deserves this. I was always taught to speak my mind. Here, if you do that, they tell you to learn respect and smack you around. How can you respect bullies? They're just sadists. They get off on seeing us suffer.

I won't let them break me, though. I'll do whatever I need to do to get out of this camp. I'm not going to let them see me cry. Even though I have blisters and my toes are bleeding and I *hate* keeping my mouth shut. I'm stronger than them. I just need to know what it takes to get out.

I never, ever, ever thought about wanting to die before I got here. I hate that this place makes you think things like that. Everyone's so desperate and unhappy. I live in a really poor neighborhood, right? But people there are full of life. They're not dead inside like here.

I'll tell you one thing, my mother is going to sue the ass off of this place. I am going to shut down this place if it's the last thing I do.

SURVIVAL CAMP, DAY 35

Rosa, dramatic
Outside, talking to her mother.

What took you so long? I didn't think I'd ever get out. I didn't think you were coming.

Is it really you? Am I dreaming this? I'm so thirsty. I don't even look the same anymore, do I?

You know what? I don't think I can walk out of here. I'm finally free and I don't think I can walk another step. But I want to leave more than anything. You won't leave me here, will you, Mom? Because I would die here. I think I would die here.

I tried to be strong, Mommy, but I failed. I didn't think anyone was coming. I didn't think you could find me. Or I thought that maybe you *did* think I was bad. That maybe you always thought I was bad. I thought maybe you were glad to be rid of me.

Take me home, Mom. Please.

RECONNECT

Rosa, dramatic
Outside, talking to a a friend.

I'm sorry. You were talking so fast. Everyone seems to talk so fast now. I just have to get used to it.

I got kind of messed up this month. I almost can't remember what I used to be like. I remember that I was loud and fun. But it's like I don't know that person anymore. I don't know who she is. She's dead. And I'm just left with this body. There's nothing inside anymore.

I had coffee for the first time in a long time yesterday. I had it because I remembered that I loved it. I thought I couldn't exist without it. And it made me sick. I'm scared. You probably don't even want to know me anymore. I'll understand if you want to move on. I know I'm dragging you down. I can't help it. I miss the old me, too.

PHOENIX

Rosa, semicomic
At school, talking to her best friend.

I never thought I'd say this, Monica, but I love this building. I love this metal detector. I love this locker. I even love Mr. McNamara, that old creep. I can't wait to sit in chem lab, not understanding a single thing.

I know it's sick! I'm sure I'll be over it in a week. But for today, I am thrilled beyond belief. Let's do something after school. *(Beat.)* I don't care what—anything! Something with lots of people around. Let's go to Times Square at rush hour and stand in front of a huge office building and let all the people push past us.

I know it's crazy, but I love this place! I will never, never, ever complain about the noise or the smell or how obnoxious people are. At least not this week! I have never been so happy in all my life! Oh my God, the bell! Homeroom! I *love* homeroom!

TAMARA JENKINS

Tamara is very concerned about how she appears to others. Very self-critical, she often finds herself lacking. Out of insecurity, she tends to mocks other to keep attention away from herself.

QUESTION AND ANSWER

Tamara, comic
At school, talking to a classmate and her best friend.

No. I'm not going with anyone. Yet. I'm just going with the flow. Whatever. Prom is not tops on my list, you know? I'm busy.

With you? Well . . . sure. Yeah. That would be nice. You bet. *(Beat.)* Sure. You can pick me up at eight.

Did that just happen, Drea? Did I . . . did he? I said yes, too, didn't I? I can't believe it! I was just so shocked I couldn't think of what to say. I just blurted it out—"You bet!" I'm such a dork.

Oh my God, I so wanted Antwone to ask me instead! *(Beat.)* Don't say that. He might have asked. You never know. *(Beat.)* I am not dreaming! Reality is just seeping in. Drea, I am going to prom with Perm Lee! The only Asian man in America with curly hair! My social life is doomed. Doomed!

MELTDOWN

Tamara, comic
In a dressing room, talking to her mother.

I can't go to the prom. Nothing looks good on me. That's putting it mildly. Everything looks ugly on me. Mom, your genes suck. I have a fat butt and I'm too short and everything is out of proportion.

It's useless. I hate wearing dresses anyway, and I can't walk in heels. Plus, I have to go with *Perm* because no one else asked me. *(Beat.)* Mom, how many times do I have to explain. He's called Perm because he's got this stupid curly hair. Can you imagine what it's like going to the prom with a guy called Perm? I don't even think I know his real name.

Let's go home. This is a bad idea.

What are you doing? I know I said let's go home, but I didn't mean it! You're supposed to tell me it's all going to work out and I look pretty. Oh my God, my life is a total disaster! Even my mom thinks I'm ugly!

SO DREAMING

Tamara, comic
At school, talking to her best friend and her prom date.

Drea, did I dream that or did Antwone just tell me I looked good at the prom? *(Beat.)* This is the best day of my life. I am going to marry Antwone Crow. We are going to have fat little babies. We are going to be in love forever!

I know I'm taking it too far, but I love him. *(Beat.)* I know he took Gina to the prom. I saw them there. And I know he's a player. But I will tame him. He is going to be my boy toy. And we are—

Oh, hi, Jeff. *(Beat.)* Yeah. I had a nice time at the prom, too. It was really nice of you to get that limo. So, bye!

How am I going to get rid of him, Drea? *(Beat.)* I know he's been really nice, but being seen with a guy like him will ruin what I have with Antwone!

OVER

Tamara, semicomic
At school, talking to her prom date and her best friend.

I'm not avoiding you, Jeff. I'm just busy. *(Beat.)* Yes, *all* the time.

You're calling *me* immature? That's rich. I am *not* immature. You are. *(Beat.)* Well, because I said so. I don't need reasons. Look, I don't like you. You're an OK guy, but I am not into geeks. I'm sure there's some girl out there for you, but you're going to have to jump off the Tamara train. Maybe try joining the Audiovisual Club. Step off now. Bye-bye!

I was not mean! He called me immature. Me! He doesn't even know what it means. He's the one wearing Dockers and argyle socks his mother bought for him. Please. Good riddance. I have got bigger fish to fry.

I don't know who. I just know there are plenty of fish in the sea, Drea. Fine, good-looking fish just begging to be fried.

THE DARE

Tamara, semicomic
At school, talking to her best friend.

Drea, did you know Jeff, weirdo Jeff with the perm who took me to the prom, is going to Harvard next year? Apparently, he got a full scholarship. I knew he was smart, but I had no idea . . .

You knew? Why didn't you tell me? I wouldn't have minded going to the prom with him if I knew he was going to Harvard. Can you believe it? Perm is gonna be rich when he grows up!

I did not blow it. I still don't like him. But maybe I should have been a little nicer, especially since Antwone still doesn't know I'm alive. What is wrong with that guy?

Antwone is not going to be pumping gas when he grows up. How dare you insult my man. If you love Jeff Lee so much, why don't *you* go out with him?

DISCOVERY

Tamara, semicomic
At school, talking to her best friend.

Come on. No way! You asked Jeff Lee out. The dork of the century. *(Beat.)* I know I said you should ask him out, but I was *kidding.* I didn't think you'd take me seriously. You were just going on and on about how I should be nicer to him . . . Are you *in love* with him? Because, I'm sorry, but that's disgusting.

I know he's nice. He took me to the prom, remember? He's very . . . polite. The kind of guy your *mother* would like. That's exactly why he's the wrong guy! Guys should be *guys.* Fooling around, flirting, trying to look down your shirt, fighting with other guys—*that's* what guys are supposed to be like. At least when they're our age. Jeff Lee is, like, eighteen going on eighty. He's practically ready to settle down for retirement. Is *that* what you want?

My God, Drea, it's like I don't even know you anymore.

LEFT BEHIND

Tamara, dramatic
At home, talking to her mother and father.

Mom, what are you doing tonight? Want to see a movie? *(Beat.)* Come on, Mom. We never do anything together. *(Beat.)* I know it's usually because of me, but tonight I have nothing to do and I'm bored. *(Beat.)* I can't go by myself! On a Friday night? There's nothing but couples there.

I can't go with Drea 'cause she has a date. With Jeff. Do you remember Jeff? My prom date? The total dork? Drea is actually going out with him. Not that I mind. He was totally in love with me, but ick. I do not like him *at all*.

I am not jealous! Don't be stupid, Mom. I could care less. But, please, come to the movies with me. I don't have anyone else to go with now that Drea is with dork boy! *(Beat.)* What do you mean, I'm the dork? I just want to spend time with the woman who gave me life—is that so bad? Just forget about it, Mom. You don't understand anything! I guess we'll never be close.

FALLOUT

Tamara, dramatic
At school, talking to her best friend.

How was your weekend, Drea? Did you have a good time with Jeff? Note that I called him Jeff instead of Perm or Dork like I usually do.

I am not being insulting. I am being the opposite of insulting. I'm trying to be nice. I can't help it if I totally don't understand why you're going out with him. I know he's smart and polite, but I don't get it. Will you cut me some slack?

Can we do something together after school? *(Beat.)* You're *always* doing things with Jeff. I thought we were best friends. We never do anything together anymore. Are you trying to ditch me?

You think I'm immature, too, don't you? Well, I don't need you. I don't need anybody! I'm going to college next year anyhow, and I'll find a new best friend. Have a nice life, traitor!

ACCIDENT

Tamara, dramatic
Outside, talking to a stranger.

I am so sorry. So, so, so sorry. Are you OK? I was just . . . I just got my license. I can't believe this. I am so dead. My mom is going to kill me. You're OK, right? Do we *have* to call anyone? Couldn't we just let it go? I mean, your car looks OK. Mine is the one that got messed up. And I *just* got my license. Please, ma'am. Please can we just overlook this? I promise I will practice and never do something like this ever again.

Why can't you be nice? I'm just a kid. I'm not a bad driver. I'm just having a really bad day. *(Beat.)* Fine! Whatever! You're ruining my life, but don't let that bother you! I have no money for a ticket or to fix this car, but don't let that stop you from calling the police or anything! I swear, your car is fine. Why do you have to be so mean about this? I'm begging you; please don't call the police, ma'am. Please!

RECKONING

Tamara, dramatic
At home, talking to her mother.

I don't want to go, Mom. I've had a terrible year this year. College is bound to be the same as high school. I don't feel like being alone. Especially since I'll be so far away from you. You're all I have left. Maybe I should just stay here. I could take classes nearby or work for a year.

I used to think I was good at making friends, but I don't know anymore. Everyone seems to have drifted away. And Drea is still mad at me. I don't know what I did wrong. I thought we were going to be friends forever.

I just know I'll have to work in the cafeteria for my school job. Mom, they're going to make me wear a hairnet.

What if I hate my roommate? Or she hates me? What then? What if she's crazy and she kills me in my bed while I sleep? Or what if she goes to parties all the time and leaves me alone? What if I have to sit in the cafeteria day in and day out by myself? I don't think I can do this. I'm so sick of no one liking me. My life is such a mess.

METHODONE SCHWARTZ

Methodone is in the process of "finding herself." Born Francis Schwartz, Methodone is very concerned about world issues and wants very much to be an individual.

REBIRTH

Methodone, comic
At home, talking to her mother.

Mom, how many times do I have to tell you? My name is not Francis anymore! It's a horrible name and I hate it! Call me Methodone. *(Beat.)* Why? I thought I explained the symbolism at the dinner table last night. It just proves you never listen to me. *Because I said so. Because it's what I want. I am not a Francis.* Francis is a horrible name for a boy who is overweight and has kinky hair.

I chose Methodone because it reflects who I am. I am dark, Mom. I'm not the cute little kid in knee socks from second grade. I put a lot of thought into this and I'd appreciate it if you respected my wishes.

If your friend Carol asked you to start calling her, I don't know, Ann, you'd do it. You'd do it without question. But with me, because I'm such a dumb kid, I get grilled like a criminal. And it hurts my feelings when you mock me, Mom. I am adult. I can make my own decisions. It's about time you accepted that, Mommy.

PAIN

Methodone, comic
At school, talking to a classmate and her best friend.

How many times do I have to tell you this? I don't like you, Maddy Lynn. It doesn't matter how perky and nice you are to me. I hate you and all you stand for. So leave me alone. I like to be alone. Why are you still here? *Go away.*

Your perkiness fills me with a white-hot hatred. It makes me want to stuff your pom-poms in your ass. *(Beat.)* God doesn't care if I say ass. I asked him last night when he begged me to stop worshipping Satan, the dark lord.

Finally! I got rid of her! That girl will not take a hint. What do you think she's on? How can anyone be that happy with all the stuff going on in the world? Ignorance *is* bliss. I wish I could be that stupid sometimes. It must be a relief. I would die to have just one day without the anguish of the world pressing in on me. I would happily donate my left arm to science if I could erase all knowledge of high school, Texas, the conflict in the Middle East, and the senseless slaughter of wildlife. If I thought worshipping Satan would help me achieve this, Scab, I would.

JUST SAY NO

Methodone, semicomic
At home, talking to her parents.

Parental unit, I cannot go to school tomorrow. The president is visiting.

I don't *have* to go to school. I'm not learning anything anyway. I choose to express my disappointment with and objection to the state of the nation by not attending.

They expect us to smile and stare in rapture at him while he blabbers on and on about how he loves the children of the world, blah, blah, blah. It's shameful! I can't be party to that, knowing what I know about how the world's children are treated by our so-called aid. We are merely forcing America's right-wing politics on other cultures! It's a joke!

No! You can't make me! I won't go! You're part of the problem, Mom and Dad, and until you see that I just can't talk to you! I refuse to see you as authority figures! Absolute power does corrupt absolutely and you are proof of it! This world is a disgusting place!

EXPECT THE UNEXPECTED

Methodone, comic
At school, talking to a friend.

Scab, what are you doing? *(Beat.)* I mean touching my arm like that. Sort of . . . caressing. *(Beat.)* No, I don't like it. Why . . . Why are you doing it?

I'm not yelling at you; I'm asking a question. It just seemed . . . weird. You don't . . . *like* me, do you?

This is weirding me out. This is completely out of nowhere. And it doesn't make sense. I mean, we're not like that. I thought we were about justice and overturning authority. And being all in love . . . it's not what we're about. It's being part of the problem. It's so *expected*. We're different. Am I wrong here?

Can we just go back to being angry now? I can't even deal with this now. My new piercing is infected, and I have a math test; I can't even think about this now.

PREJUDICE

Methodone, dramatic
At a store, talking to a stranger and a store clerk.

What are you looking at? Take a picture; it'll last longer, lady. I swear, you are so rude. Excuse me for not buying my clothes at the Gap. The American Dream: You too can be just exactly like everyone else and have no individuality inside the big, American melting pot. God bless America!

I will not leave this store! I have just as much right to be here as anyone else. *(Beat.)* I am not disrupting anything! If someone was rude to you, you wouldn't let them get away with it. I am simply telling this obnoxious woman to mind her own business.

You go ahead and call security. What are you going to tell them? "There's a woman here speaking her mind! Come take her away immediately before she gets anyone else thinking!" You're all mindless drones.

Did you just call me "little girl"? You are trying to repress me. Make me feel small. I am too large to be contained by you and your small mind. I am outta here, *ladies*.

CRISIS OF FAITH

Methodone, comic
At home, talking to her family.

I have decided to become an atheist. Starting today. I realize this will mean no Hanukkah gifts from this point forward. I accept this. Especially since you seem determined to give me the same things you buy for Lauren, which I do not want anyway. What made you think that I would want a pink shirt with the word "Princess" spelled out in glitter on the front?

Well, I reject God because if He or She exists, this divine being clearly hates me. I mean, a Princess T-shirt? If there is a holy force at work here, I . . . I just don't know what to say. This shirt is a clear example of how the universe is in chaos.

Don't ignore me. I'm making a point here. You'll ask me later why I'm doing this, and I don't want to have to explain again. *(Beat.)* I know you want to have a nice day and it's a holy time for you. I'm not trying to ruin things. In fact, I want you to know that I respect your religion. I do. I am just forced to reject it entirely based on your heinous, total disregard of all *I* believe in, in the form of this top. That being said, I am going to my room. Good day to you all.

OCTOBER 31

Methodone, comic
At school, talking to a classmate.

You think I look *nice* today? Nice? This is my Halloween costume. I'm dressed as a brainwashed lemming, aka the American teenager. Personally, I am freaked out. I don't know how you can live like this every day. I feel as though I'm seeing my reflection everywhere I go. I look exactly like everyone else. It's hideous.

That's offensive. No one looks like me today. I don't dress like a Halloween ghoul. I dress how I *feel*, but you wouldn't understand that. It expresses how I am on the inside. When *I* dress, I'm not trying to impress silly *boys* like the media wants me to. I don't care what anyone thinks of me. Especially you.

I'm "cute" today. Gee, thanks. Is that supposed to make me feel good? Is that meant to make me conform? I'm not going to make myself approachable so you feel better about yourself. You can just forget it, Mr. Normal Guy Loser.

PRETEND

Methodone, dramatic
At home, talking to her little sister.

You miss me? That doesn't make sense. I'm right here. Shelly, you're too little to be sad. So just stop it.

OK, fine, I'll bite. What's wrong? *(Beat.)* Nothing's different now. Everything's exactly the same. That's the whole problem. No matter how many days pass, everything seems exactly the same. And everything is boring. I'm the same, too.

I still play with you. I know I used to more, but I'm busy now. I'm not a kid. I can't just be happy and fun all the time. When you get older, you'll see the world is not a happy and fun place. You're just a little kid. I wish I could go back to being where you are sometimes. I'm in a totally different place now. Can you understand that?

OK, fine. I'll try. I'll pretend to be happy and fun for a little while, but just 'cause you're my sister. I don't do this for everyone, you know. So stop crying, it's really making me sad.

THE TIDE

Methodone, semicomic
At school, talking to her best friend.

Scab, do you ever think this is hard work? Being like us? I think I probably spend more time dressing than all the girls I make fun of.

Sometimes I get tired of being so complicated. Worrying about other people's problems and what's wrong with the world. Sometimes I just want to have a pizza with pepperoni and mushrooms and not think about how I'm eating an animal and how farmers are being exploited. Do you know what I mean? I probably shouldn't have said this, but I just want to get it off my chest.

You agree? Well . . . we can't go back. I made such a big deal about being called Methodone. I can't just be plain old Francis again. Then everything I've done will be a joke. Everyone will just think it was a silly teenage phase I went through. I still believe in all the same things, though! I just don't feel like fighting all the time anymore.

We've gotten ourselves stuck in a mess, haven't we? If we stop doing this, we'll just be weird, fake posers. As long as we keep going, at least we seem to have values. God, do you know it takes me, like, a half hour to take off my eyeliner? Having beliefs sucks.

RE-REINVENTION

Methodone, semicomic
At home, talking to her family.

I just want everyone to know that just because I'm not wearing black eyeliner anymore doesn't mean that I'm not angry or sad or horrified at the state of the world. I am. This is a sick, demented planet, and I will forever be objecting to the misuse of authority. Just because I look more . . . like everyone else doesn't mean I have given in to the pressures of society. So don't be all happy about how your little girl is back to normal or anything. You should probably still be ashamed of me.

And I'm Jewish again, even though there's lots of things about it I don't like. Don't hug me, Mom! I'm making a statement. This is not a happy day. This is a miserable day like all others. Only I'm not wearing eyeliner and I'm Jewish. Just those two things. Everything else is the same.

I just found that my rebellion was taking on a pattern that was also disturbingly clichéd. I will be seeking an entirely new, individual way to express myself from now on. I just don't know what it will be yet. But it will be so-called weird and wrong, so I'm just telling you now to brace yourselves.

THE AUTHOR

Kristen Dabrowski is an actress, writer, acting teacher, and director. She received her MFA from The Oxford School of Drama in Oxford, England. The actor's life has taken her all over the United States and England. Her other books, published by Smith and Kraus, include *111 Monologues for Middle School Actors Volume 1, The Ultimate Audition Book for Teens 3,* and *20 Ten-Minute Plays for Teens Volume 1.* Currently, she lives in the world's smallest apartment in New York City. You can contact the author at monologuemadness@yahoo.com.

SMITH AND KRAUS, INC.
MONOLOGUE ANTHOLOGIES FOR MIDDLE AND HIGH SCHOOL

Girls Speak Ages 13–15: Sixty Original Character Monologues
Boys Speak Ages 13–15: Sixty Original Character Monologues
Girls Speak Ages 16–18: Sixty Original Character Monologues
Boys Speak Ages 16–18: Sixty Original Character Monologues

Great Monologues for Young Actors: Vol. I
Great Monologues for Young Actors: Vol. II
Great Monologues for Young Actors: Vol. III

Multicultural Monologues for Young Actors
Short Scenes and Monologues for Middle School Actors

The Ultimate Monologue Book for Middle School Actors:
   Vol. I: 111 One-Minute Monologues
   Vol. II: 111 One-Minute Monologues
   Vol. III: 111 One-Minute Monologues

The Ultimate Audition Book for Teens:
   Vol. I: 111 One-Minute Monologues
   Vol. II: 111 One-Minute Monologues
   Vol. III: 111 One-Minute Monologues
   Vol. IV: 111 One-Minute Monologues
   Vol. V: 111 Shakespeare Monologues for Teens
   Vol. VI: 111 One-Minute Monologues for Teens by Teens

Monologues in Dialect for Young Actors (dialects included:
   Russian, American South, New York, Standard British, Cockney,
   and Irish)
Scenes in Dialect for Young Actors (dialects included: Russian,
   American South, New York, Standard British, Cockney, and Irish)

To order, call toll-free 1.888.282.2881 or visit our complete cata-
logue online at www.SmithKraus.com.